Pinky.

by Kaitlin Marianne

Pinky.

ISBN: 978-0692154038

Printed by CreateSpace

Cover by Clara Tennant

To all those who have ever touched my life—
you have shaped me in ways unimaginable.

Thank you.

Dream

don't blink, I whisper—
you don't want to miss anything
not a single moment,
a single ray of golden light
pouring through the window pane
on a chilling winter morning;
touching this face,
mouth tipped open,
eyelids fluttering;
you don't want to miss a single eyelash
for they hold millions of wishes
yet to come true;
you don't want to miss
the gentle rise & fall of his dainty chest,
the covers draping over him—
a bed of new fallen snow
on the steepest of mountains:
delicate
captivating—
it's these moments
I find myself happiest
to lose a few moments
dreaming

Water Dance

We dip just the tips of our toes
into each new crashing wave,
wary of the force
and bracing ourselves for all that could come.
This archaic dance
of overthought steps
left us fearful of mistake
and tentative of everything new;
every new wave brings a new battle
that we tip-toe around,
knowing there are more on the way
and that we'd never want another with whom to face;
The waves grow furious and strange,
dark and ravenous,
frequent and scary
and I wonder how we'll manage
dipping my toes in,
performing this dance,
all piles a heavy weight on me—
and yet, I still want no other
but you.

Poison

Simplicity
is the word
that drips honey on my tongue one instant
and pours blood the next

Sweet and Menacing

and
in the end of it all
I know that simplicity—
though there may have never been
a sweeter sound—
is a poison to all
greater underlying complexities
I hold
unrevealed.

Want

How do I know
What I want
When I want it
If I am ever
Like the Weather?

Color

Life lacks its luster in hues black and white—
Give me Golds rich as marigolds
and Greens bright as the stems
upon which the buds are perched;
give me Peaches, Strawberry stained lips
and Sky Blues stretching for miles—
How wonderful it is to have this world
painted just for me
through sounds
pressed keys
bird chirps
and the spots on a newborn doe;
an entire world appearing as all my own
with rose tinted sun lighting
shining on a verdant meadow—
a lush hideaway
to escape.

Need

Oh, how I long to cherish myself
as you have me—
To cradle myself in my own arms
and feel the myriad of constellations in my heart—
To see my own duality
and welcome it with warm wakings.

Pathways

There once was a boy
with a head full of snow
who dreamed about tigers down below;
He wished and he dreamed,
and though all it could bring,
There were not any tigers to show—

There once was a girl
with a head full of shells
and a bucket of fears she wanted to quell;
She puffed out her chest,
and tried very best,
But few washed away with the swell—

There once was a pal
with a head full of blooms
whose petals could take an entire room;
They didn't get why,
and began to cry,
For millions of eyes brought their doom—

There will be a time
When we all blur the lines
Between all of the You's and the Me's—
The wants that we deem,
and the fears that we beam,
And happy is all we will be.

Baby Breath Reverb

pinkies interlocked in undeniable truth
baby breath bouncing from blanket to cheek
— is this what longing is?

                              baby breath reverb,
                              cheek to cheek—

More

How can I be special?
With only 26 symbols to my native tongue—
only so many sounds sewed together
cannot hold all of life inside of it.
How can I speak of something new
with only one tongue
to wrap around all syllables untold,
to unfold this life compacted in front of me
when there are concepts in others
that burn my tongue like ice
the moment I begin to remold myself to feel
them brushing inside my mouth agape in awe—
Where there are more words for love than lust
and more words for life than survival.

Night

red neon
depth of night
clear air
24hr lives
fluorescent skies
wired souls
shaky breath
hands bold
long drives
short glance
dance of fidgets
endless chance
lips red as roses
& roses red as lips
wild hearts
burn for more

One Day

my artillery of words
will be home to every combination of letters
that know how love feels
I am home to heart's swell and
one day
I will be home to their brothers and sisters
too

Skating

My body, the warmth of you—
tender and kind
heart to heart
skin to skin;
Figure skaters, gliding in rhythm—
frozen cheeks
flowing bodies
flushed hearts

You

The one who calls me art
doesn't realize
How badly I wish to capture their essence
in a glass jar—
lighting up a single piece of artwork
laid upon a bed of plucked grass;
an impossibly complicated task
for someone so complex
and captivating,
brighter than any hue
laid behind
by the stroke of my brush

Name

my name is not my own—
perhaps it was lost
and tossed in the lost & found,
only to be wrongfully taken
and shoved into my gentle,
trembling hands,
embroidered into my skin,
blood leaking through impetuous stitching—
it aches.
my name is not my own.

Waiting

Waiting—
Waiting for lightning to strike me in the head;
For the heavens to open to me and sing,
Blaring all trumpets and horns through the clouds;
For happiness to come in,
Perched on the clipped wings of angels in golden sandals;
Waiting for divinity to take over for me
And give me hits of magic through wind chimes
And a full life through breath alone.
Waiting, always waiting—
not Feeling, Loving, Dancing,
or Doing
But just waiting
until time caves in
collapsing on my hollow chest.

Ink

I want my words
to be stained with ink
and the tears of knowing finally
Someone has felt
as You feel
and with this ink
overlapping Our skin,
We understand the importance
of trying to begin
once more

Fears of Mine

there's nothing I fear more than solitude—
an existence desolate and lonely,
composed of watching dust fly,
freezing to the core;

But
I know
that even without other hearts,
I always have my own;
and I intend on making her,
that lovely soul and kind spirit with the aching heart,
all of me

Push

thoughts swirling in my skull
ideas brewing in my brain
all signs pointing towards
no limits—
endless destinations
endless journeys
endless sunrise
endless pains

Sharing

I'm so thankful to be able to share with you
the silliest of body parts—
like our (lanky) arms
and our (clammy) hands
and our (candy) lips
                all dangling,
                      and draped,
                            and pressed,
                                  and entangled
what's yours is mine
and what's mine is yours:
a pinky promise I know we'll keep.

Lifetime

11:33 pm
how do you trust the process
when it doesn't trust you

11:34 pm
my time is up
my skin is burnt
— empty

11:35 pm
how strange
to find comfort
in the arms
of someone I don't know

12:06 am
you are the warmest being
I have ever known

Childhood Bedroom

the one place that remains the same
while everything else: a whirlwind of change—
warm lights
cool sheet
mounds of pillows
and mountain peaks

ceiling tethered stars
and music boxes so faint;
disheveled towers of books
and chipped down paint

a room filled with growth:
vines growing out windows
all dreamy and dreary
with shadows below—

Merrill Park

meadow stained clothes
smelling of fresh cut grass
and green sunshine
blue skies and cotton candy eyes
wind carrying dandelion puffs—
a paper boat in an unpredictable sea
waves in and waves out
Childhood is found here

Pinky Promise

do you remember
you were stuck in Boston
and I in Philadelphia
319 miles between our bodies
but nothing between us
do you remember
you went for a walk
on worn cobblestone sidewalks
enveloped in the darkness that is 2 o'clock
wishing to be swaddled
forever in this blanket of darkness
I clutched onto your sweatshirt,
the closest physical distance would allow,
willing you to a brighter path
beyond the bridge
do you remember
staying on the phone
breathing heavily
drawing yourself back to your nest

always will I use everything I have
lifting you up
when all you can lift up
is your pinky
promising me that you will try
another day.
with a simple linking of pinkies,
we are bound
with breath
and the promise of new mornings.

Trust

chest ablaze with desire for the future
as bright and burning as the flame
trailing in the distance.
things take time
itching for something yet to be built,
nearly forgetting to build,
remembering to build—
you mustn't slacken your reign on the ropes.
to escape
lay trust in the foundation
found within your bones.

Base

expect not your greatness
to spring from a home waging war on you
it stifles and stops
Overcome
And find all that is waiting for you
in cherry picked blossoms.

Loss

Before loss,
there is always losing;
Before moss,
lack of sunlight oozing—

Rot

I am filled with rotting
and this pit in my center
filled with sludge
bubbling and grueling
I am filled with haze
up to my eyeballs
brain stinging as it is scorched through the day,
hot sun of desert sands and tumbleweeds—
bleached bones
eyelids drooping because there just isn't enough strength
to go around
losing myself in these dark corridors
filled with dust
so bleak
you only fear once you close the door again

Storm

trapped in this whirlwind
the gusts picking up
unrelenting
seemingly
until they crash—
and I with it

The Morning After

a long drawl
a puff of smoke
hazy and lazy and blurred
the arduous lullaby
goes on without being sung
the words piling up
thick in my chest
pressing into lungs
I'm not quite sure are mine
leaving microscopic cracks
for oxygen to slip through

slowly,

but surely,

it will run

out

it always

does

A

there is no sweeter taste
than that of your name
dancing around my tongue
safe and precious
molding to the concaves of my mouth
and rolling through my lips,
unwilling to let go

Sunshine

You are sunshine because I pour all of my rays into you—
You and all of the other You's there have been
and all of the You's there will be—
it has made me a burnt out star
who has collapsed in on theirself
falling out through the sky
aimlessly—
while You— and all the other You's—
stay put
endlessly burning
bearing the task of lighting the world
as I wither away into space dust—

Crinkle

crinkle paper
crinkle paper
crinkle from the other side
I can't believe
you still can't trust
after all this time

Share

You tell me you care
But don't want to share
Your heart in the both of our hands,

Yet you want to take mine
Just any old time
For the same exact feelings we shared.

If you do want a kiss,
But miss out on the bliss,
There's no care anywhere near—

You want a blow out of sight
While nothing's alright;
Try to tell me you care
While you continue to use me
Night after night.

My body is not a playing field—
It is home to a brain and to love.
It is not something greedy hands take—
It is home to all wonders above.

So if you kiss me, that's fine
but just know in due time
I will expect for your heart
to also be mine.

Last

minutes later
my lips still buzz

hours later
and you are still there

months later
will I still feel you?

years later
will you still haunt me here?

You and I

You and I
are so numb
lose control
but just for fun
salty breeze through cotton blue
a part of me is a part of you

You and I
were so young
to be tormented
for so long
golden streaks
upon your face
a part of you has left a trace

and I am so afraid
of everything you said yesterday
you were mine
and I am yours
but we are no more.

Light

all these blinding lights—
puffs of smoke until you're out of sight
you love me, but not tonight
draped in silk and silver moonlight
face never fades in the light
I'll forget, but not tonight
then you're lighting up the sky
lighting down the highway
tonight

Growing Pains

I have growing pains
but not of the legs
or feet
or arms
or tongue—
I miss my mother in times lacking slumber—
growing older grows harder
because of these growing pains of the heart.

Waking Up in the Morning

glass half full or glass half empty
maybe it's all empty
maybe I'm sitting in a dimly lit room
with only a sliver of silver light even trying
to sneak in out from under the blinds
to draw me out
to snap me back
to draw my eyes away from the blank
empty ceiling
with not even a whirring ceiling fan to keep me company
to be a companion
to numb me
to have everything,
every sensation slip away from my mind and from my being
the sunlight hidden behind the blinds
waiting for me
my once comfortable bed sheets are now composed of
nothing at all
floating in an empty glass
somehow never ending

maybe if my glass were half empty

or even half full

life would feel like something,
be filled with something

like life

instead of emptiness

instead of nothing at all—

Promises

promises, promises break
promises keep
promises break
when you break
the promise you make
the person you keep
instantly breaks

Ghost Pains

how must I forget you
when each time I reach for my book
I am reminded of ways in which I am bound to you?
I flip through and see sketches of you
and flip through and see poems
and flip through and see these vivid fractals
painted before me
an entire film reel
of our lives together
and flip through and just wish with everything
to bathe in that once again
and flip through and feel my hand buzzing
where yours was
and flip through and feel where your lips have been
and flip through and feel your entire body
pressed to mine as we'd dream together in the nighttime

So here I am
pouring you into these pages
to try to rid me of you—
yet as the pages fill—
so does the reason to linger
as I give myself another thing to flip to
when you're gone
to feel everything draped over again

Trade

and the glitter smudges on my face
and you have left your trace
I trade a piece of me for a piece of you
everything came from out of the blue
never should have sunk into
neon reds and haunting truths

Sand Slips

I have felt everything
from your hair between my fingertips
to your fingers tapping mine—
now sand slips through my fingers
and there is no more time

Time Stills

clouds of dust thicken my room
light streams in just enough
to see each particle float
I hold hands with my despair
as we lay wrapped, cocooned in quilts
your face nears mine but I can't return
I'm not sure how much longer this means
for you and me

Unchosen

How do I say goodbye to my Muse
whom I didn't choose
and watch as he leaves me for good?

As he leaves, does he take the art with him
or, in a way
is he here to stay
burned into my skin
for the rest of my days?

For at the end of the day
when I sit down to play
it is still somehow him
who ends up on my page.

Antithesis

pink rockets in the sky
bubblegum and winter fourth of july
love streaks through blue hues so white
horrid antithesis of lover's delight
it all fades to navy
and lightens to black
in your bountiful hope
that I never come back

Nov 1, 2017

I at first dated this Oct 27 without even thinking it
I guess I am stuck in the past
on the way to the train station, I smiled genuinely
for the first time in 2 weeks
I began to skip as I was so giddy
I actually felt light, even weightless
as I was carried up to the sky by bubbles
because somehow, suddenly, the weight bearing on my chest
lifted
and sucked all of my body weight in with it
just for a few instances—
then later I boarded my train
and all that weight crashed down once again
as I was stationary
in a body moving forward
breathing became heavy
feelings sprung up all too familiar
feelings that hold qualities similar to water—
they feel so fucking heavy poured on top of you
but somehow you just can't live without it
everything is dim and I am stuck as you propel forward
my eyes are heavy
my head is heavy
everything,
everything is fucking heavy
young and done, in despair
trying desperately not to care

Just as
you did.

Bare

Everything in my head gets unbearably loud. all of this noise creates so much pressure in my chest, making it feel like a balloon with too much hot air stuffed in it. I can't release it unless I shred my lungs or breathe deeply and when I do, I pop. my flesh feels like the wrinkled rubber of a party balloon that's lost its purpose. losing sensibility. losing myself feels like driving through a thick layer of fog on slick asphalt during the most ambiguous hours of the day.

It is hot and it is numb as you lay me bare. bare to fend for myself and bare to search for missing pieces through days built by haze. yet again, everything pours into my head to fill it with hot air, threatening to burst before I even have the chance to collect my most intimate pieces and trinkets and soar.

Thunder

Do you remember when all of our biggest fears
were Thunder?

clammy palms, cold sweat
stabbing fear in your chest
keeping you from leaving your safety net?

What happens when you are expected
to protect someone from the very thing
that you most Fear?

storm clouds striking in your chest,
organs with lightning,
shaking your body,
thunder distending in your uneven,
unpredictable breath?

How can I protect you from what you Fear
if I can't face it myself?

I grab my armor and get up anyways.

I swallow the Thunder
I strike back at Lightning
I dry the rain
I stay out of hiding

thunder battle bravery comes blissfully
when the sake is not of my own.

Sound

And so goes the age old question:
if a tree falls in the forest,
and nobody's around,
does it make any sound?
to which, I wonder:
if I ignore everything—
if I build up barriers of steel
between myself and my Torment
is It still there?
is the heavy sack of pain
I am prone to carrying on my back
still waiting for me?
or did It just vanish?
disappear?
give up?

no.

It is waiting there,
waiting to punish me—
waiting to strike back at me
for ever even trying to protect myself.
It is not just waiting but breaking down my shield,
ripping it apart with razors for teeth
and shears for arms
bringing everything to crash down into the grass
surrounding It
so dry and dull yellow it is now hay,
a shell of what it was—
ever trying to feed off the bosom of the sky
for nourishment
growth
strength
purpose—
but the creature with blood in Its eyes—
and blades everywhere else—
Its sight is set on me.
the blood stained dagger that It clutches so easily
as if it were Its favorite pen;
the dagger I know all too well
ready to plunge deeply in me
like a familiar greeting
from a relative who left me trembling on Christmas Eve
but who always came back the next year.

Yes, that tree makes a sound—
and I'm sure it's just as ready to pounce ravenously
into the ears of anyone who is around
to be taken advantage of.

Allergies

cherry lips
peach pit
nature's candy
makes me itch

coffee eyes
honey skin
how can we
ever win

Breath

air is viscous
clinging and compressing my lungs
breathing once light and simple
has instead become like drowning
the flood of my ribcage
rising, sweeping houses away,
to release through ducts
unclogged

Coping

if I just write
until my wrist cracks and aches
maybe I'll find beauty
amongst shaky handwriting
while the ground crumbles away
beneath all that matters

The City

the city is dark as our thoughts
the eerie quiet numbs
swallows
suffocates
wrings out the hope it can
letting us drip dry
each drop
slipping and dripping
far too quickly
hitting the pavement
losing shape
shattering
as the handles are in their hands
and the garrote pinches our necks
making us lose the only thing
we've ever truly known
nothing is more chaotic
than the stark silence
rooted in fear
but
underneath
our people hum
sweet songs
of revolution—
once a mere whisper
but growing evermore;

Blue Goldstone

You still wear bits and pieces of me,
blue and glistening,
gifted, right on your ribs,
as if you are as proud of me now
as you once were
So please tell me
with every single word you own
why that is not true
like you make it seem

End

my eyelids have become weights
pressing deep into my skull,
painting the skies black,
bruising it with amethysts and emeralds
and millions of atoms begin to tremble
one by one, they crawl together
and form you—
sadness drips from me
as sunshine pours out of you
beyond me
the rainfall pokes at the glass unceasingly,
the constant crackle loosening the locks—
everything is no more;
just dark grey clouds tinged with yellow—
the lingering trace of golden sunshine.

Manifestation

I will hang my sentiments on a flagpole again
raise them highly with conviction
boldly and proudly
only this time
They will not quiver.

Balanced

The most blissful times in my life
have all occurred in the brief few moments
When the moon and the sun
have joined each other in the sky
for their evening tea party.
They both shine on opposite sides of the checkered cloth,
neither one overpowering the other.
Everything feels right—
Harmonious, even.
Perhaps we could learn from them
sharing the water from their tea kettle,
dunking tea bags and eating lemon cakes,
coexisting
just as beautifully—
just as naturally.

Fleeting

that feeling
you sit in grass
far too overgrown
and the sun peeks out from the clouds
prickling & tickling your skin
then disappearing behind a cloud again,
playing hide and seek tag with sunlight—
the sun is everfleeting as we are;
reminders of fleeting existence—

Lemons or Limes

right person
wrong time
but is it such a crime
if you look for a lemon
and get a lime
happens all the time

Tune Up

The air conditioners turn off and you, for an instant, experience deafness as your ears acclimate to the quiet. Beyond your head, beyond your brain, beyond the snoring of the dog lying next to you, beyond the fogged window, cicadas and crickets continually chirp such as bits and pieces of a brass orchestra tuning their instruments eternally.

This is what home has always sounded like.

Buzz

I used to run from bumble bees
For fear that they would sting,
But now I melt into the stoop
For flowers they will bring;
Bees want buds
And bees want flowers
And bees don't have time for me
In their few short hours—
I watch the honey
As it drips from their homes;
They are not here to hurt,
but rather, to roam.

Wherever

Be wherever you are
for time is ever ticking
and moments ever fleeting
and each one
whether it makes you ache
to the point that you begin to shake
and the night curdles,
the darkness thickening, black slime
seeping through the corners
and every crevice and break
to engulf you whole
to the point that you lose yourself
Or
whether it makes you light
to the point that your mouth creases into a smile
and the happiness that dwells in you
begins to bubble and boil
in your gut
in your very core
and travels upwards

up
up
up

until each one bursts

                    pop
    pop
              pop

And you are fizzing

like your favorite drink
from your youth
because in this moment
it feels as if
the childhood you longed to live again
never stopped—

Feeling, on its spectrum,
on its very intricate spectrum
never ceases, no matter
where it falls
whether in a deep dark pit
or on a park bench in the summer time
as time is taken from our fingertips
so
Be wherever you are
cherish each moment conscious
for they are how we learn to be human,
finding peace in our souls
and homes in our bodies
Truly just—

learn to be okay with that.

Passion

Keep stars in your eyes
The burning sun in your heart
And you will go far.

Inspiration

inspiration
does not always come
strapped to a firecracker
bound to explode any minute;

sometimes
it comes in shades of grey
when the world is just barely at your fingertips
and your breath is soft

no explosion—
no sudden revelation;
it forms over time
like a seed grows to eventually flourish

it was always there
developing, unnoticed
embedded in you
under the pressure of the millions of lives you've lived
becoming a diamond

Drain

I watch in despair
as all of my memories
get dragged down the drain,
my feet cemented to the floor—
I'm unable to fold over
and scoop you back up in my arms;
I barely graze you and I
and light pulls out of my chest
through lengths of my arms
and straight out my fingertips
and goes down the drain as well.
I am suddenly empty
and my innards feel like hell.

I am expected to watch you go
and pour down the drain,
entangled in clumps of hair
as it all rips out;
yet I can't seem to believe you
when you say "*it's for the very best*"
with your soap water mouth.

Work of Fiction

I am a work of fiction
here for you to write all over,
tear up and tear through with red ink
dripping between lines of pages
which will eventually be slashed through
and through,
eventually reworded, reworked, and revisited yet again,
awaiting that wonderful day when I am finally complete—
but you realize in all of your perfectionism and obsessive ways
that this labor of life will never be as you want it to be
that the slash marks on the pages are eternal
that the rewrites and reworks will always be
in perpetual motion
and that you will never be able to complete this,
try as you might—
You may fill me as you like
with all your red marks and underlines;
but just know that I will never be put to rest,
published for the sake of others.

Preschool

I must unstick myself from you
like in preschool
pulling back glue
from the ridges in my skin—

sitting on my favorite orange circle on the story time carpet
time passes when you're all that matters

Dust and Ashes

it all became a wasteland the moment you left
my feet drew up dust;
the ground was nothing more
than the ash of all who came before.

trees are warped into knots from years past—
hollow, weakening, splitting fibers;
grass plucked out like eyelashes,
dry and ragged

the world is grey.
and perhaps there is nothing I can do to change that;
perhaps all that's left is not to salvage the land that was,
but to learn to love the land as it is

perhaps through this love
of my grey, desolate world
Perhaps then I will see more flowers bloom.

Comfort

what does it feel like?
to cry in the arms of someone that loves you
whilst all alone
smelling of baby powder and rain
amongst the dim ember glow,
tenderly shattered
and put together
again

Deal

Dearest,
I am immensely proud of you
for extracting yourself from your sheets,
a place far more familiar to your flesh
than the entire world waiting outside.
every day, you make a choice
and today,
you chose yourself
despite the overpowering current dragging you back
and drawing you in
you chose yourself—
you chose me
and you chose recovery.
and I can't thank you enough.
I'll try to take care of you
if you try your best to take care of me
—deal?

Jewels

I miss you more
than I wish to say—
latching onto sapphire days;
a spark, an end, and now dismay—
oh, how I wish
the spark had stayed.

Stick

I wear loneliness like an old jacket
I just can't seem to get rid of,
or like a distorted perfume that refuses to go down the drain
as I rinse my skin to remove every trace
with fruitless attempts

Still

I see you still on warmer days
I see you still with skies ablaze
I see you still in boxes of fruit
I see you still in begging for proof
I see you still in new fallen snow
I see you still in handwritten hello's
I see you still perched on my lawn
I see you still because you haven't gone.

The Current

Paddling through rough waters,
Pushing forward into the lights
Piercing through the layers of crashing molecules
Waves lap up against you, encouraging you towards light
Suddenly you break through; waves no longer crash on you,
They bump into you gently, barely noticeable
Somehow, you didn't see this change
And you didn't notice the light growing stronger as you
Reached these gentle waters
You realize that there is so much more
Than constant stormy weather and rip currents
There is floating and there is calm
There are new seashells, there are sand dollars
And there is so much more waiting for you beyond
The current

Happiness

perhaps we are only as happy
as the happiness we give others—
or maybe our happiness
is a solitary force
but, either way.
What matters is that happiness exists
just as much as the grass on our lawn
or freckles on your skin—
The clouds in the sky
and the deer in the woods;
And it may not be in you yet
But someday, it will be
And you will feel the warmth
From your golden glow
Permeating through everything you touch.

First Moments of Peace

hushed lights grow
blue drapes blossom
streetlamps glow
across petal clad pavement
warm orange rays
change to cool blue breeze
life swirls around
the oldest of trees
it smells like the beach
with none in my sight
memories buried
within simple delight
goosebumps raise
and hair starts to stick
one deep breath
each day to pick
birds scurry
night flurries
relief all in sight
day after day
and cotton cloud night

Metal Vent

the first time I was left home alone
I was 11 years old
cheeks red like tulips
or constant sunburn
skin even more milky than now
hair plastered and untouched
a crash—
and suddenly I am a shadow
trembling nauseous dizzy
hiding in my mom's closet
with a cordless home phone
tucked away in my pocket
the door's closed, I awaiting the monsters behind the noise
sure to appear in the form of beastly men
who want nothing but torment for young ones such as I
I await my impending doom with organs lodged in my throat,
wanting to call mom to save me but knowing
that the slightest peep will clue them to my whereabouts;

minutes later
the front door opens and familiar voices waft through
the air
as Pavlov's dogs drool, my heart lightens and energizes
I kick down doors and bound down the staircase,
blazing by the banister
I leap into the arms of my parents
they point my awareness to the tears stained
on my cheeks
I explained the crash and thus the obvious invasion and
the knots in my stomach
I explained detailed depictions of what the perpetrators must
have looked like, reliant on the sound
(either woodland creatures made of tree trunks or burly men
with unkempt facial hair and biker jackets)
Then my mom found it
the perp
a metal air vent that had come loose and fallen to the floor
my nerves, though still in bunches, further began to quell
one of my first experiences as an adult
riddled with childhood nightmares
forced my letting go of the fantasies in which I lived.
I have spent my whole life since
navigating the pleasure of safe fantasy
and childlike creativity
that won't allow my petrification over harmless threats
not just the metal vent
but of all the creatures I thought it were as well.

A Sense of Realism

Nothing is "realistic"—
The more we limit ourselves to this fake sense of realism,
The more we limit our minds
And negate all prospects of progress.
The point of being alive at all
Is that both nothing and everything
Are realistic—
Even the most absurd of things—
Just by way of existence at all.
I challenge you to not think realistically
Or to acknowledge that true realism is anything and everything
simply because
it exists in any capacity at all
in our headspaces and in the air
Fuckin' anything, anything at all, can happen.
So why limit yourself with just one silly word
When your possibilities are boundless?

It Only Rains

and it only ever rains
these days when I think of you
it only ever rains
a cold rain
a rain that freezes you into the center of your bones
surpassing further each layer of our own carcass
not even any longer the warm rain of the humid summer
down pouring to seek relief
from the heaviness it has come to know
through the thick underbrush of night
you have become freezing rain
sometimes we grow to know that even those we know best
we no longer know
when I think of you, it only ever rains

Vessel

I am a vessel.
People pour themselves in me and
transport themselves through me.
People love me and people love to use me.
People then are able to see themselves in me.
People only love me once they fill my hollows
with themselves, their secretions contained
within my physical barriers, my
mental limitations.
These such boundaries, however, are seemingly
inexplicably limitless.
Yet they somehow are so very limited.
There's only so much of you, all of you,
I can take before my fragile bounds burst.
Before each shard of glass only shatters further to oblivion.
While I am aware that my existence is for
the sake of others, I can't help fantasizing
of if my breath could ever be for the sake of my own.
Or if my hollows could rather be filled not with
the likes of me, but with me, wholly and fully.

Is it possible for I, this vessel, to be anything
more than such?

Is it possible I could be not that which
I always thought I was?

Is it so that I might be more?

More than empty, containing all others' hearts
and fractures,
more than a paper boat
carrying flowers torn from roots
floating along aimlessly
in a grotesquely captivating fashion?

Or is this as good as it ever shall get—

Is this as good as I ever shall be?

Imperfections

I find comfort in my pages
smelling of pasts I can't remember
laced with wispy handwriting
faded markers
underlined notebooks
once too afraid to ruin
and now too afraid to never have lived fully

The F Word

used to burn those in my community;
will not be used to burn me.

And if you dare try
I will burn you right back
with the force of a thousand stars;
then, maybe, you will step back
and think about those flaming branches you toss out.

Brand New

I let go of you through ways
of clutching onto myself
missing you has been as the tide
controlled by the moon's pale light
and the phases of each day
intricacies and complexities
all piled high in these sticky mounds for sandcastles
either knocked down immediately
or left standing to see a few more hours
I pad across sand so cold and damp
trying to stick to my toes
while the waves reach out to me
to fold me in its gentle grasp
but for the first time
they only manage to catch ahold
of the footprints that I leave behind
and for the first time in months
untethered to the sea
I collect seashells
for myself
I adorn myself with these gemstones of the sea
clouds part and light reflects off of their wet bodies
colors of violets and bright orange creams melting,
becoming one in a fresh, saccharine light

each step I take from you
each breath that is wholly my own
of the lemongrass scented breeze
each day further away is another shell
another piece of ocean glass
strewn through my hair
pressed on my skin in makeshift freckles
and piercings without the pinch
breathing in and feeling mysticism inside my ribcage
fluttering salt breezes and the intensity of a 6am sunrise
red, bright, renewed, and hopeful
the fresh air is clearer now
clouds no longer of the mind now adorn the sky in a faraway land
I do have the pleasure of not seeing this morning
here, today, it is clarity all around
ice on your tongue, full night's rest, lack of pressure behind the
eyes kind of clarity
no stuffy noses, smelling grass for the first time kind of clarity
upon self-reacquisition, life becomes brand new
brightly.

Still Growing

I am grateful to be alive, to breathe in fresh air, to be able
to go outside and see the sky and walk on the grass and
feel the cold prickle my face and I'm grateful for the sun
and all of the trees and for colors changing in the sky and
I am grateful for puffy clouds and barren trees because
it reminds me of all of the room there is to grow. It is okay
to start from nothing, barren like the trees, or even small
and vulnerable like a sapling that needs wooden supports
to keep it held upright, kept from folding underneath the
pressure of itself.

You will grow as the leaves do. It is gradual. You don't see
it happening, but one day you will feel full and look back
fondly.

Remember to be ever patient and gentle with yourself.

You are still growing.

Complete

I am my own beauty
I am my own love
I am my own god like figure
sent from above
I am my own spark
I am my own rage
I am my own purpose
through my dying days
I deserve this life
and I deserve this air
I deserve the whole sun
to be my own gentle care
I will feel complete
once found the missing piece
but it is already breathing
and living through me

Quiet

My hand still holds onto your shape
as if you will come back another day.

What scares me most
is your time to go
was swift and painful
and no one knows.

My ears like to ring
so they feel less alone —
This is a shallow
and empty home.

Songs of Summer

melodies floating
through my soul
like wisps
blown from a freshly picked dandelion
carried by a breeze
through the warmth of a summer sky
painted
with sidewalk chalk
scented of fresh cut grass
and endless nights
keeping myself company
in even my loneliest days

The Divine Feminine

how dare you try and silence
The Divine Feminine?
how dare you shove your finger
where it doesn't belong
digging into My parted lips,
coated with truth
and glossed with gold?
for I am anything but complacent—
I am constantly moving.
constantly growing.
constantly pushing through your barriers
to protect My fellow Divines.
My open heart and expanding mind
are alike in their infinite capacities.
My words are whips
encrusted with candy crystals—
I am powerful,
I am ethereal,
I am glistening with hope for The Future
and raging with knowledge
and the will to spread it.
how dare you expect silence to pour out of Me
when I am anything but?
how dare you assume
that you have the power to dictate
everything that I am?
that you can just lay out broken stepping stones
into a forest full of deafening snarls
and rusted razors
and that I'll follow that step by step
into your greedy trap?

how dare you reprimand
honesty
and
justice.

I am The Divine Feminine—
I am here for all of my fellow
Divine Feminines—
and They are here for Me—
and We will paint the town
gold
from the tips of Our fingers.

We will be anything but silent
for your comfort.

We are loud
We are outspoken
We are passionate
We are unstoppable because
We are unified
Our Voice
Our Heart
Our Soul.

how dare you expect complacency from The Divine Feminine.

Reflections

like a rose
bathing in moonlight

//

she is like a rose
bathed in moonlight

Deep

and I never knew of
unconditional love
until I found myself
deep within yours—

lush and fragrant
as the morning stills,
taking me in
while rolling down hills—

red and bright
as the tail of a fox—
and all the patience it takes
to hand stitch wool socks.

Bloom

A lonely little flower
In a field all her own
Still struggles to find
A true sense of home;

Her petals have wilted
And her energy's drained,
Making her feel
A new kind of pain;

"Why are there no others like me?" she wonders
And upon that lingering thought
She ponders and ponders;

"If others don't grow as I have,
It's alright" she proposes—

"As long as I grow
To be more than I need
So that I can be
Happy ol' me."

So the next time it rained
And her world filled with drear
She took in that water
And proclaimed *"I belong here!"*

And she repeated that mantra
Every passing day
'Til her petals sprung up
And energy soared away

And a weak little flower
She was no more—

She grew taller and brighter
As every stem should
And she was all that she needed
To feel adoringly full.

After

like a human
starting small,
growing tall

Trapped

in this sheet of glass—
I see a canvas
light as day
tinted pink
through a rose colored peephole
and with light pink polka dots
all speckled across the sky,
playing connect the dots for bubblegum constellations
on a complexion of pink moonlight—
I see soft, yet vibrant, pink lips
crowned with cupid's most precise bow—
and I see unruly golden spirals
shooting out from whatever angle they please—
and I see unruly eyebrows
that dress two deep-set eyes,
drowning in pools of plum's pigment
reflecting a glimmer of hope—
and,
my, oh my,
is that artwork
trapped in the glass
a beautiful sight
to be set free—

Sip

I sip on the universe
as if that will fill me
with the likes of you:

all of your purpose,
and beauty,
and truth.

The milk of the milky way
replenishing the earth
drips down my tongue—

unfolding, I see
all our worth
left unsung.

Bubbles

there is nothing like the joy   *
     of seeing your dearest friends
tugging your heart strings
     until you burst   *

        (and out come the bubbles!)
 *
                     *
    *
           *
  *

Presence

I can't stop thinking about your face all ablaze
when I called you wonderful the other day.
It is true, you are full of wonder
and I of wonder for you;
for I go through my days
and not remember a thing
but you—
every detail, every last ding;
the scar near your mouth,
the twitch of your lip,
the roundness of eyes,
my grip tends to slip.
never in my life have I been
this comfortable and this nervous
all in one trip.
butterflies in my chest,
forbidden, though perhaps just a sip;
mind wanders to you and fingertips long to brush—
how can all of me ache so much
when there's still so much unlearned,
all spoken in flourished whispers.

you've begun to appear in my dreams
and each time I wake
I feel the bliss
of waves crashing against my bare chest,
sunlight so warm it bathes you more purely
than perhaps the water ever could,
kissing my skin and painting me as it pleases.
I have become yours
and you have become an exquisite force of universe
present in my mind
I shall write for you day in and day out;
from my mouth love shall spout.
You and I in the sky:
fading waves, crystalline moonlight

Bug Bitten

bug bitten I'm smitten
bug bitten I'm itchin'
bug bitten I'm prayin'
that you'll go away

it starts with a bite
and ends with a swell
with hopes that you're gone
by the end of the day

Vanilla

her laughter smells of warm vanilla
and I am enamored by her
who knew a heart could beat so fast
until the moment I met her

I can't help but feel what I can't
I can't help but dream of her eyes
I can't help but wish for her hand
I can't help but plead for more time

I dream of her as I enter the folds of my sheets
I remember daintily her touch of my cheek
maybe she is lust like many say she must
but maybe she is stardust
and it is enough.

Crick

We head down to the creek,
But you called it a crick —
And the crickets would chirp
Perched up on their sticks;

The sound would surround
And the creek would be bound
To the edge of the world
In which we are found;

The birds start to chatter
As our movement makes clatter;
Our toes dance and swing
Through clear water they shatter —

Air gets swallowed by night
But we don't lose our sight;
Nymphs and fairies come out
And we know we're alright.

They dance through the brush
And sprinkle their dust;
It gets in our eyes
And allows us to trust—

Your hand goes in mine
While we walk through the vines—
The vibrant moonlight
And fingers entwined;

The whole world is yours,
Yet you say it is mine—
We could share one another
And spend all of our time—

Summer days by the creek
That you still call the crick—
Each and every adventure,
I wish them to stick.

Q

I always knew
my favorite letter was q
but I didn't know why
until I met you

Love

how do I know that I love you?
is it known because I say the words
or because of the never ending shutter on you
or how every color always looks best on you?
is it known by proclaiming it
or by picking all the wildflowers that remind me of you
as a gift?
is it known by money spent
or by our adventures and misadventures taken?
if time were coins it'd be spent on you
the flash will go off
and we both will light up
and I will love merrily with you.

Pride

I do not entirely feel
as you have molded me—
why must others dictate
our most fundamental parts
when we can find them
for ourselves?
your dictation has trapped me
has limited me
has made it harder for me
to explore the artwork I am.
I am different
and I am art
and I still find it in my heart
that I am Proud.

Apples

streets are paved with gold
but we carve through them;
the apple doesn't fall far from the tree,
so I hold its core in the grip of my hand;
they say we will be so happy in 20 years
but why not now—
I had a pet newt named Marius growing up, who I saved from
death
I would do anything for Marius— slimy, scaly Marius
it was valiant to others but not to me
it was love to me
why do others see it as a selfless act— a grand gesture—
and not as love, the simplest of intrinsic human qualities—
the apple doesn't fall far from the tree
but what about the two trees that grow closely together,
their branches intertwining with age, gnarls and spots appearing
to wrap them closer, still
blooms coming and going with seasons change
what about them
their unwillingness to move
their roots planted in the ground
their sureness that even with age and weather, nearly nothing
will take them down
what about those trees
where the apples just don't fall

Protected

You grabbed my hand in the protection of night,
Unsheathed by way of green tinged streetlights—
But will you hold my hand as proudly as now
In summer's fairest daylight?

Chosen

My family
is not composed of blood
linking all of our veins
through the red string
sewn through arteries
hanging from one to the other
a clothes line of genetics;
It is all those
who lifted me up
when up sprung the pain
and those who stayed
when time passed slowly our days.

The Exact Taste

I love to say the word sweetly
and taste the sugar on my lips
as our lips part
and peaches and cherries find themselves together once again
moving like fluid
air catching and erupting
momentarily parting the parted mouths
longing for each other's tenderest touch
soft and wet breaths caressing my face as well as your hands
hands I have found that are smaller than mine
my back dimples with the surge of your touch
reaching northward towards my neck
my head to folding back
sugar drips inside my chest and thus
sugar drips
I feel what you long for in each trace of your finger on my hair
follicles
each individually standing, hoping to bide for your sole attention
what you want is as I want
in this realm we are only separated thinly by nacreous clouds of
inhibition and reaction
hope and despair
longing and fulfillment
candy in the air

we look up at picturesque moon paintings,
the hieroglyphics of our loving mother,
laying in shaggy carpet
and hearing deafeningly the entire world's buzz
amidst the slight separation of our bodies
until you roll over on your side to gaze upon me
and I do so to you
lost amongst sweet crystals once again,
your breath making me hazy as your lips once again
comfort mine
your hand once again finding home amongst my ear
neck
and cropped haircut
you cannot hide all that you feel despite the darkness
I know through your caress and your touch the depth
to which you feel
that you long for the same sweetness as I
that I send ripples through your flesh
as you have mine
that I am trickling down inside of you
that though I am new
I am the exact taste

Baby's Breath

baby's breath,
blooming cheeks—
with you I'll spend
my endless weeks.

Green

You asked for the glimpse into my mind—
and thus, to the lock of my heart;
my face was heated
and my hand searched for yours;
in these brief moments of you
wishing to know the inner workings of me,
I fell deeply in a pond of love, green
surrounded by moss,
lily pads,
and weeping willows
all weeping for the next moment
you long to know me

Sunshine pt. 2

Sunshine, Sunshine, where did you go?
Sunshine, Sunshine, I'd love to know
a pit of black tar wherever I go
I need to find where the light glows.

I travel far with packs on my back,
pockets with blankets and warm colored snacks;
I reach for my foot, pry it out of the soot,
and trudge on to see the adventures afoot.

I crawl through the mud,
the rain sprinkles my neck,
fingers dig into dirt
for one grueling trek—

I narrow my eyes,
bite the inside of my cheek—
For finding what's missing
I mustn't be meek.

I hoist myself up to the top of the peak
and overlook valleys that all seem so bleak;
Then all of a sudden I feel the warm glow,
then see how it shines not far down below—

With questions wrapped in my brain
and breath trapped in my lungs
I peak down at myself,
gasping through tied tongues—

That warm glow, so bright it lives like sunlight,
Shining outward and high, splicing the sky;

To my wonderment and surprise
and through teary eyes
I realize that I am the sunshine
for which I've searched all this time;

If your sunshine has up and gone:
do not fret and do not moan—
For everything you love is exactly where it belongs—
From you it will come, For you it stays known.

Thank you.

Index

Acknowledgements

Thank you to everyone who has believed in me throughout this entire process— this help has been absolutely indispensable.

Thank you to Clara for the beautiful cover design and for reading and finding joy and inspiration within my pages. You helped bring this book to life in a very real and tangible way and I am so grateful for you.

Special thank you to Mia and Rebecca for being the first two people ever to read my book cover to cover (before it was even bound to a cover). Thanks for letting me write down every single thing you said and for sharing this moment in time with me.

Thank you to everyone who has supported my work and let me send them the things I have made, to those who have said that they would love to read my work, and to those who believed in me when I told them all of the things that I want to accomplish.

And thank you to my family members who, upon my telling them that I was going to publish a book, said "that's pretty cool."

This is for you.

Find your happiness and run with it—
and thank you for supporting me running with mine.